The
Blessing And Losses
We Share

NAILAH ABDUS-SALAAM

authorHOUSE®

AuthorHouse™
1663 Liberty Drive
Bloomington, IN 47403
www.authorhouse.com
Phone: 833-262-8899

Published by AuthorHouse 03/19/2021

ISBN: 978-1-6655-2052-2 (sc)
ISBN: 978-1-6655-2051-5 (e)

Library of Congress Control Number: 2021906101

Print information available on the last page.

This book is printed on acid-free paper.

Bismillahir Rahmanir Raheem

In the name of Allah, the Gracious, the Merciful

All praise is due to Allah. We praise Him, we seek His help, we seek His forgiveness, and we seek refuge in Allah from the evil within ourselves and our evil deeds. Whoever Allah guides, there is none to misguide him. Whoever Allah leads astray, there is none to guide him. I testify there is no God but Allah alone, without any partners, and that Muhammad, peace and blessings be upon him, is His servant and His messenger.

The truest word is the Book of Allah and the best guidance is the guidance of Muhammad. The most evil matters are those that are newly invented, for every newly invented matter is an innovation. Every innovation is misguidance, and every misguidance is in the Hellfire.

"Actions are by Intention"

Umar Ibn Al-Khattab relates that he heard the Messenger of Allah, *sallallahu 'alayhi wa sallam*, say, *"Verily actions are by intentions, and for every person is what he intended. So the one whose hijrah was to Allah and His Messenger, then his hijrah was to Allah and His Messenger. And the one whose hijrah was for the world to gain from it, or a woman to marry her, then his hijrah was to what he made hijrah for."* [Agreed upon]

Acknowledgements

I give all praise to Allah The Creator of Everything for His guidance, and granting me the ability, the patience, and perseverance to finish this book.

I want to thank my family who were supportive in my time of loss and throughout this endeavor. A special thanks to my great nephew Jared Suggs who is becoming an excellent photographer. His photo was selected for the front cover of my book. You can find some of his other photography on instagram @flashfreeze.jared

And to all my "sistahs" out there who gave me encouragement and support during a difficult time. Jazakum Allah Khair.

Contents

Introduction xi

Part One   The Testing 1
               Poems 3

Part Two   Grief 15
               Poems 19

Part Three Reminiscing 23
               Poems 25

Part Four   Acceptance/Hope 31
               Poems 35
Part Five

               Coping / Acknowledging Divine Decree 43
               Poems 49

Closing 63
About The Author 67

Introduction

This book is written by a Muslim woman as she worked through her own grief after the sudden death of her son. O my friends. I never hoped to write this book, but here it is.

It is infused with just about everything that has been present to me in the wake of my son's death nearly a year ago. Inclusive in the ache of heartbreak is the hope, the sadness, bewilderment, the beauty and grace, the consistent patience & prayer needed, and the unrelenting love that is intertwined on each page. I have included several Hadiths, quotes, poems, Ayats that speak to losing someone and overcoming the loss, as well as the joy from the countless favors & numerous blessings we all share. We have so many blessings, and as we move through the anguish, we are rendered into unexpected shelters of solace and hope. Shimmers of light that help us see we are not alone. Those who know loss will find kinship among these pages. We remember our loved ones with both tears and laughter, and these poems contain the wholeness of being human. I hope this book has the ability to comfort, as well as speak directly to your heart.

Most of all, this book is a gift from my broken yet hopeful heart to yours.

Part One

The Testing

Life is a journey from Allah to Allah.

Be *sure We shall test you with something of fear and hunger, some loss in goods, lives, and the fruits of your toil. But give glad tidings to those who patiently persevere. Those who say, when afflicted with calamity, 'To Allah we belong, and to Him is our return.' They are those on whom descend blessings from their Lord, and mercy. They are the ones who receive guidance."* (2:155-157)

Tests, Trials, and Difficulties

Whoever Allah wants good for him, he puts them to test. He puts them through difficulties. Like a diamond or some metal that has to be burnt and then that which is bad from it is removed so that you have that which is the pure diamond or the pure gold or whatever. [Tirmidhi and Ibn Maajah]

- **There is wisdom in every test.** The world (dunya) is not the resting place, It is the testing place.

"**Happiness is attained by three things: being patient when tested, being thankful when receiving a blessing, and being repentant upon sinning.**" **[Imam Ibn al-Qayyim (rahimahullah]**

Inna lillahi wa inna ilayhi raji'un- (To Allah we belong and to him is our return.') May Allah, forgive our loved ones and make their grave wide and full of light. Aameen...

Prophet Muhammad (peace and blessings be upon him) said: "If Allah wants to do good to somebody, He afflicts him with trials"

[Sahih Bukhari: Volume 7, Book 70, Number 548]

- "When we are not able to change a situation, we are challenged to change within ourselves."

  Abu Hurayra reported that the Messenger of Allah, may Allah bless him and grant him peace, said, "Remember frequently the thing that cuts off pleasures," i.e. death." [at-Tirmidhi]

Poems

IN THE STRANGE

One week later in the strange
Of losing my son.
The strangeness surrounds me.
JANANZA
I receive instructions
Of how this jananza (funeral) will be.
A couple of friends,
And only a few from the family.
No visitors at the hospital or the cemetery.
All this because of Covid 19.

No time to mourn yet,
Too many responsibilities.
The cool winds blow right through me.
Awakening to the empty spaces,
Surrounding me.
The planes soar high overhead,
Scribbling a message in the clouds,
Saying he is gone, he is now dead.
.Many have died this day,
Many people have gone away.
The cemetery is full of bodies.
No more time,
This is a sad ending.
This world and everything in it,
Is only temporary.

WITHOUT YOU

Things won't be the same,

Like they used to be.

We won't sit and talk any more

Under the shade of the oak tree.

No longer will we see,

The beautiful sunrises over the heads of you & me.

Forever cherished memories,

Many layers & complexities.

No longer will we see the vivid sunsets,

No longer will you be reminded,

To live a life without regrets.

No minutes, no hours, or days,

Can make anything change.

This world is only temporary.

Disappointments will one day disappear,

I've already shed a lifetime of tears.

I hope no one else comes to know,

The pervasive agony of woe.

There are no holes in the ladder of despair,

Better days are coming,

I hope I'll soon be traveling there.

CORONA VIRUS 2020

Our lives changed overnight.

None of us could have predicted,

How our movement would become so restricted.

We met loneliness in isolation,

So much confusion & uncertainty in this situation.

Rarely see loved ones & friends,

No longer is there face to face communication.

This virus has no discrimination,

And it's spread beyond and throughout our nation.

People losing jobs,

In a state of desperation.

Graduations were canceled that should have been celebrated.

I know pain doesn't just go away.

Rather you're outside or at home is where you'll stay.

If you have lost someone who is precious to you,

Take their dreams and the words they spoke,

And wrap them in your heart a covering with hope.

This test hasn't come to stay,

I pray we all live to see another day.

As for the goodbyes we never get to say,

We can still hold them in our hearts every time we pray.

The love that was there,

Won't fade away.

THE LONG GOODBYE

She's still my mother, who's standing there.
It's still her eyes, her face, her hair.
It's still her body, but it's just a shell,
of the mother I once knew well.
The fabric of her memory has slipped over time,
Her vacant stare details her confused mind.
A likely irreversible decline.
Alzheimer's is stealing my mother away,
And she's getting dimmer with each passing day.
Images of life's events worn down,
Memories like shadows, falling to the ground.

Thoughts disappearing on everything,

No longer able to think deeply about anything.

It started ever so gradually,

With small changes in her personality.

She's become adept at hiding,

Just how bad it's all getting.

Just to utter some words is becoming agonizing.
A myriad of things she is unable to say,
Like fingerprints,
Where no two people experience it the same way.

Some days are good,
While others are bad.
Her mind is clouded and confused,
As she tries to assimilate the words she chooses to use.
Sometimes she's lucid and it seems to have disappeared,
She tells her stories,
So adamantly and clear.

Now I'm having difficulty distinguishing,
What's fictional and what's real!
Bits and parcels of memories cease to exist,

It seems like I haven't had a regular conversation

With my Mom, since 2006.

She no longer understands, and she strikes out at me,
Masking the devastation of this reality.

Oh my dear mommy,

I want you to remember how you once loved to cook.

I want you to remember how you once loved reading books.

I want you to remember your loved ones' names,

I want you to still enjoy those monthly card games.

And all the other things you once loved,

And the joy that still remains.

Her possessions tell her story of who she was,

A wife, a mother, a grandmother,

Whom we all loved.

I remember vividly, so clearly,

How she fought to save each memory individually.

But now her thoughts are unraveled,

And run randomly.

Diminishing her abilities and reasoning.

Robbed of her memories and history.

Dementia distorts relationships,

Where there once was intimacy.

She is present,

Yet she is absent to me.

She tries to remember but the gate is closed,

The key is missing, and the lock has a bolt.

In our isolation,

There is often a quiet communication.

Her smile always gives some indication,

She is still here.

She is still the person I hold so dear.

Alzheimer's is a thief that steals your personality,

This illness has stolen the mother who birthed me.

Her mind is like a book already read,

Where a page is torn out every day,

Until the whole book disappears away.

What happens to each passage as it disappears?

Tethered stories of all those years.

What becomes of our collective journey?

Her stories merge with mine.

Even in these devastating times,

There's still layers of love

That only the soul can define.

UNANIMOUS

Let us agree
That we won't allow ourselves to say,
This breaking makes us stronger
And the pain will go away.
Would it have been better to never know his love?
Then to feel this deep wound,
That awakens me almost every day.

CAN WE AGREE
It's better to go through the pain
Because without his love
Life would not have been the same.
The whole point is to continue to love,
From the richness in which it came.

PATIENCE

Be Patient

In your test & trials

Be Patient

With the people's harm.

There's no trial,

Except that you can get through it.

There's no test,

Except that you can get past it.

Whatever trial comes your way,
Know that it will go away.
It may not even last one more day.
Be Patient!

Sabr (patience) enables a Muslim to demonstrate reliance and contentment to the decree of Allah. This will also allow the person to be grateful to Allah despite such loss knowing that Allah will never burden a soul with more than he/she can bear. This pivotal moment will be rewarded with something much bigger in the future. Observing patience does not mean we cannot feel saddened or cry out of our grief; for Prophet Muhammad (peace and blessings be upon him) also had tears in his eyes when his son Ibraheem passed away. But we don't take it to extremes such as hitting oneself, crying loudly & excessively, tearing and ripping our clothes, and we don't question Allah's decree. These acts are strictly prohibited. We don't want to waste away on the great reward that is to come for being patient.

Part Two

Grief

Allah does not burden any human being with more than he is well able to bear [2:286]

Grief is a journey that must be taken. The experience of grieving cannot be ordered or categorized, hurried or controlled, pushed aside or ignored indefinitely. It is inevitable as breathing. It may be postponed, but it will not be denied. We lose people in various ways: When they die, through illnesses, in wars, homicide, divorce, when they move away, through separation, mental illness, and sometimes when they choose a different path. Loss is Loss. Sometimes you may see them again, sometimes you'll never see them again. Life is a journey from Allah to Allah.

You will be fundamentally changed by your loss. Others have too. It takes time to discover who you've become. Realize that each person is different and will grieve in ways you may not understand. During your time of sorrow, bring your family together. Be patient and find ways to support each other. Sadness and anger need to be expressed and released. Sorrow can be so heavy and paralyzing. . As much as you might want to "shut down," it is usually very helpful to try to keep up with your daily life – go to school, or work and go out with a good friend. And finally, it's always beneficial to take good care of your physical health while coping with grief. You might struggle with this thought, but grief, sadness, and anguish can be a blessing. The reality is that you won't grieve forever. You will not 'get over' the loss of a loved one; you will learn to live with it. You will heal and you will rebuild yourself around the loss you have suffered. You will be whole again but you will never be the same.

Allah, the Almighty says, "And it may be that you dislike a thing which is good for you and that you like a thing which is bad for you. Allah knows but you do not knows". [2:216]

- Life can be inexplicably hard. Bless every present moment.

- People may say, It wasn't his time,
  But that's not up to you nor I.

- Yesterday is gone, you have no idea about tomorrow,
  So why ruin the beautiful present in yesterday's sorrow?

- For every happiness, there is a moment of grief that follows it; and every house that was filled with joy, will sometimes be filled with sadness.

- There are times you have to immerse yourself in the grief, so you can cope with the loss of a loved one. Grief can hang around. It will follow you wherever you are. It can become your companion days and nights as it lingers for a while. Embrace it, you can't out run the process of grieving.

- **A tear that runs down a believer's cheek is more beneficial than a thousand raindrops on the earth. [Ibn Qayyim Al-Jawziyya]**

"When Allah tests you it is never to destroy you. When He removes something in your possession it is only in order to empty your hands for an even greater gift." [Ibn Qayyim Al-Jawziyya]

"There is no joy for the one who does not bear sadness, there is no sweetness for the one who does not have patience, there is no delight for the one who does not suffer, and there is no relaxation for the one who does not endure fatigue." [Ibn Qayyim Al-Jawziyya]

Verily those who say: "Our Lord is Allah (Alone)," and then they remain upright (Istiqaamah), on them the angels will descend (at the time of their death) (saying): "Fear not, nor grieve! But receive the glad tidings of Paradise which you have been promised! We have been your friends in the life of this world and are (so) in the Hereafter. Therein you shall have (all) that your inner-selves desire, and therein you shall have (all) you ask for. An entertainment from (Allah), the Oft-Forgiving, Most Merciful.

[Quran 41:30-32]

Poems

LIFE IS FLEETING

In the emptiness is all.
So we must learn to embrace it all.
Now is only temporary.
The trouble with the present is,
   It's always in a state of vanishing.
    This worldly life is fleeting.
   It is here where I lay down the burdens
    Of the mothers before me.

COLOR ME BLUE

Blues surround us in the day
And in the night skies.
I Am Blue
Blue as a ocean
Crystal blue
Like the bluest sky
Caught in the clouds of blue.
I'm resting in the heralds of winds blew
From a vibrant sapphire to a blue misty hue.
My garment is blue
My khimar is blue too.
Wrapped up in blue
Veiled in a midnight blue.
When suddenly out of the blue,
My mood changed,
I praise Allah melancholy didn't remain.

ON THIS LONGEST DAY

He crossed over
In the evening countless stars appeared,
And suddenly it couldn't be any darker,
Or any more clear.
Each moment became longer and larger,
There's no more catching one's own eye in the mirror,
Mirroring me, mirroring us.
This day doesn't get any realer.

CAN YOU STAND THE RAIN

You'll never see a rainbow without seeing a little rain,
You'll never experience joy without some residuals of pain,
No matter how difficult things may get,
Keep moving, because you haven't seen the best yet!
Better days are coming,
After hardship comes the relief,
Always stay covered under the Umbrella of Tawheed!
And may your loftiest deeds be lifted high,
Like blossoming rainbow petals,
Adding color to a sunset sky!

I THOUGHT I SAW HIM

Sometimes I would see someone from behind that looked like him,
But when they turned around,
I realized it wasn't him.
Sometimes it wasn't and sometimes it was.

And now when I see someone that looks like him,
I'm ready to rush over and hug him.
Until they turn around, and it isn't him,
And I realize it won't be him.
Never will it be him again.
I think I need a change.
A place where when I turn a corner,
I'm not tempted to call out his name.
And I'm not reminded on every turn,
That things will never be the same.

TEARS LIKE WATER

Tears, Idle Tears
Why do they come?
Or they of sadness or of things left undone?
Tears of acceptance rise in the heart,
And gather in the eyes.
Idle tears falling, as the heart cries.
Sometimes they are the best unspoken words,
That the heart speaks.
Tear tracked lines rolling down the cheeks.
Tears glisten laced with pain,
Until this anguish no longer remains.
Tears that cast a shadow on the heart,
Only dark listening to dark.
Every tear like the summer's rain,
Each teardrop speaks,
But none the same.
Like a torrent rush,
They continued to gush.
Tears that open the heart to the depth,
Until no tears are left.
Crying out all the darkness,
All the loss and pain,
Continuing to call on Allah
By His Most Beautiful Names.
She used tears like water,
Forcing their way to the light.
Until the darkness was gone,
And the sun shined bright.

Part Three

Reminiscing

Life is a gift from God. Our children, family, friends, neighbors, and even strangers are all gifts to be savored. Although some days may be full of hardship and sadness, with each breath, and each heartbeat, It is a demonstration of the beautiful gift of life. Hold on to the positive memories. Choose positive memories over regret, choose love over sorrow, forgiveness over anger, and peace over anxiety.

And thank God for the blessings in your past, present, and future.

Al-Hamdulilah Rabbil Alameen.

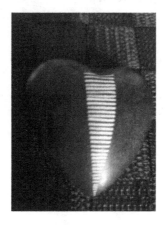

- There is a sacredness in tears. They are not the mark of weakness, but of power. They speak more eloquently than ten thousand words. They are the messengers of overwhelming grief, of deep contrition, and of unspeakable love.

- Life is not guaranteed at all, but death is absolutely guaranteed upon all, yet we still prepare for life more than death.

- Those who have gone before us, cannot steady the unrest of those to follow.

- The world is 3 days: As for yesterday, it has vanished along with all that was in it. As for tomorrow, you may never see it. As for today, it is yours, so work on it." [Hasan Al-Basri]

- <u>This wordly life is like a shadow. If you try to catch it, you will never be able to do so. If you turn your back towards it, it has no choice but to follow you."</u>

Love brings love while regret leads to discontentment. Let the death of a loved be a lesson of detaching from this Dunya and to hold Allah (glorified and exalted be he) in your heart above all others.

Poems

REMINISCING

I sat in silence at the beach
I wrote your name in the sand,
but the waves came crashing in
And suddenly washed it all away.

I used my pen to imagine
Writing your name in the sky,
but the wind just blew it away.

I carved your name into a tree,
But your name eventually faded away.

I wrote your name in my heart,
and that's where it will always stay.

EVERY NOW AND THEN

Every now and then
My smile disappears and I linger in thoughts,
Holding back tears.
Overcome with sadness feeling like no one is there,
Then I remind myself that I'm in Allah's loving care.

WE WEAR THE MASK

I don't know what to do with all these feelings,

I'm praying this is a step towards healing.

Hiding our feelings and shading our eyes.

We wear the mask,

Like a disguise.

While our hearts bleed inside.

At least we look happy,

While we grin and smile.

No need for the world see our swollen eyes,

From all the tears that have been cried.

We tell ourselves in sha Allah this will pass,

Surely this range of emotions can't last.

Sometimes our eyes perpetrate what's going on in our lives,

So we wear the mask, it's a suitable disguise.

PATIENTLY WAIT

Personal events will become interesting again.

Blossoming Buds will be lovely again.

Your passions will return again.

Your smile will return again as your friend.

Hobbies will return to being fun,

You'll soon enjoy days out in the sun.

Fall foliage will return to hues of color,

No longer a sad face reflecting in the mirror.

You will surprise your own self,

When a good hearty laugh exits your mouth.

For happiness will return unexpectedly,

Even pain will become interesting.

As it ebbs and flows,

Life will make sense again.

That enormous emptiness will fade,

To open up to brighter days.

The hours will be filled,

Their memories will last.

And the memories will be positive thoughts of the past.

RAINDROPS

Go out, take a walk in the rain.
Rain drops wash away your pain.
Feelings flowing so deeply,
Even the flower petals are wet and weeping.
Let the rain touch you,
Stand in the rain,
It's a sunnah act to do.
Make abundant du'a too.
Enjoy the sensation of the raindrops falling on you.
Rain is from Allah's bounty,
And a mercy from Allah the Al-Mighty.
So use it as a blessing.
Appreciate the goodness and gift of rainfall,
A gift that has been given to us all.

REPETITION

The mind repeats,

What the heart can't delete.

A love succumbed to defeat,
Is too heavy a load,
And hinders new blessings,
Waiting to unfold.
Honor the space in between,
The no longer and the not yet seen.

Don't spend your entire life
Collecting all the world's treasures
Death awaits us all
The destroyer of all pleasures.

LINGERING MEMORIES

The moon lingers a moment over the house,

Before it disappears to the unseen.

A cool night turns foggy,

Yet the moon continues to beam.

My mind,

My heart,

Is filled with so many memories.

Stars are descending,

Each one individually.

Life is strife,

The world is always changing.

Life is not like a portrait,

Forever remaining.

Soon we all will be leaving.

While we have time we can still love,

Give love completely!

Part Four

Acceptance/Hope

"Verily, with hardship there is relief" (Qur'an 94:6)

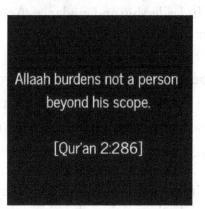

Allaah burdens not a person beyond his scope.

[Qur'an 2:286]

The Messenger of Allaah -sallAllaahu alayhi wa sallam-said:

There is no one from among Allaah's servants, who is afflicted with an affliction except that he says: "Indeed, we belong to Allaah and indeed to Him is our return. O Allaah recompense me for my affliction and replace it with something better than that".

{Inna lil-lahi wa inna 'ilayhi raji'oona, 'allahumma'jurnee fee museebatee, wa ákhliflee khayran minha}

Except that Allaah compensates him in what he has been afflicted with, and gives him that which is better than the previous thing.

[Hadeeth taken from 'Saheeh al-Kalima at-Tayyib', By Shaykhul Islaam Ibn Taymeeyah

- **Bear with patience whatever befalls you."**
  [Qur'an 31:17]"

- **"Only those who are patient shall receive their rewards in full, without reckoning."** [Zumar 39:10]

Accept that your loss will offer you a new understanding. You can survive and thrive. Trust God with all of your thoughts and feelings, even the negative ones. If you are struggling in your faith, cry out to Him. Accept His leadership and guidance. Accept His peace and comfort and be an instrument of His will.

'No calamity befalls on the earth or in yourselves but is inscribed in the Book of Decrees - (Al-Lauh al-Mahfuz), before We bring it into existence, Verily that is easy for Allah'. [Qur'an 57: 22]

> "And if something (bad) befalls you, do not say, 'Had I only done such-and-such, then such-and-such would have happened, rather say: *Qadrullaahi, wa maa shaa' fa'ala* (This is from the Qadr of Allaah, and He does whatever He wills)." [Muslim]

The Prophet (sall-Allaahu 'alayhi wa sallam) said: *"There is no affliction which strikes the Muslim except that Allah* (subhanahu wa ta' ala) *expiates with it (sins), even with a thorn that may poke him."* *(Bukhaaree & Muslim)*

- Hopelessness mocks memories and empties the future of possibilities.

"Whoever loves to meet Allah, Allah loves to meet him, and whoever hates to meet Allah, Allah hates to meet him." [Source: Sahih Muslim 157, Grade: Sahih]

Every soul will taste death, and you will only be given your [full] compensation on the Day of Resurrection. So he who is drawn away from the Fire and admitted to Paradise has attained [his desire]. And what is the life of this world except the enjoyment of delusion.

[3:185)]

"The parable of those who take protectors other than Allah is that of the spider, who builds (to itself) a house; but truly the flimsiest of houses is the spider's house;- if they but knew." [29:41]

Poems

THE AFFAIRS OF THE BELIEVERS

In the Dunya
There is no stability
Life is full of fragility.
Yet everything to the Believer is a bounty.

One passes through wealth and poverty,
Tranquility and on-going difficulties.

One passes through strength and weaknesses,
One passes through health and sicknesses.

One passes through alternate periods of happiness and dismay,
Spending time doing what's needed,
Not just out for fun and play.

In good times and bad times,
A believer turns to Him in total submission.
When dealing with any type of affliction.
Remaining patient through any hardship,
With a firm conviction.
Amazing are the affairs of the Believers!

Ibn Abi al-Dunya mentioned that Prophet Dawud (pesce be upon him) asked Allah, "What is the least of Your blessings?" Allah revealed to him, "O Dawud, take a breath." Dawud did so, and Allah told him, "This is the least of My blessings on you."
— [excerpt from Patience and Gratitude by Ibn Qayyim al-Jawziyyah, pg. 70]

FALLEN LIMBS

A limb has fallen from the family tree.
Branches lost, so hold on to good memories.
Remember the best times,
And surely the sun will shine through.

A limb has fallen from the family tree,
The quiet after they're gone is deafening.
One day more branches will be added to the tree,
Remind my children of their lineage and ancestry.
Until that day,
Remember they are a part of you and me.
Continue family traditions, no matter how small.
Go on with your life, don't worry about me at all.
Always make Du'aa that Allah guides them all.
.

MULTIPLE TRUTHS

When you experience trauma or tragedy,

You will reflect & recall innumerable memories.

You will have moments of joy, sadness, anger,

And feel guilty.

Conflicting emotional states,

Sometimes they come simultaneously.

Multiple truths just reminiscing.

Mixed feelings co-existing.

Grateful to be aware of this knowing.

OPEN HEART

Hurt breaks the spirit,
And no one can soar,
When the heart is ripped open once more.
Living now with a broken spirit,
Hoping joy will pay me another visit.

I am learning how to live
in a new way.
Ever since that day,
You were taken away.
I am learning how to live
by embracing the pain,
Knowing that you live on
Through the memories that remain.

The best laid plans are sometimes altered
through circumstance.
Trying to remain encouraged,
Hoping happiness is given another chance.,

NAVIGATING LIFE

Navigating the terrain in our daily lives,

Some lose their way,

Wakening in the morning as a Believer,

By night fall,

They stray.

Some don't see the blessings in another glorious day!

Some lose so much time,

Some lose their mind,

Some lose their souls.

Some lose hope,

Some just can't cope.

Some lose their personality,

Life has afflicted their identity.

Some lose themselves,

Some lose wealth and health.

Others live in a state of hate,

Feeling there is no escape.

Some question their lives and fate,

And some renew their faith.

Let us be of those who renew their faith.

Rasul Allah (sal Allahu alaihi wa sallam) said that Allah said: "I have prepared for My righteous servants what no eye has seen and no ear has heard, nor has it occurred to human heart." [Bukhari]

In other words, Jannah is better than anything you can imagine. Our human experience does not prepare us to imagine how wonderful it could be. "And no soul knows what joy for them (the inhabitants of Paradise) has been kept hidden." [Al-Quran 32:17]

THE TIME BETWEEN TIMES

Your life in the present,
Is in between the past and the future.
What has preceded can be rectified by repentance,
And seeking Allah's mercy and forgiveness.

As for the future,
Rectify it with firm resolve and true intentions.
This is something that won't tire you.
Rather it is an action and from the things you can do.
.This is a firm resolve and intention of the heart,
Which will give rest to your body, heart, and thoughts.

Life in the present ...
Is the time between two times.
If you rectify these two times,
You will be successful,
And achieve a blissful state of mind.

COMFORT OF THE SEA

The rise and fall,

The *synchronicity* of it all.

The rush of love,

The surge of grief,

Struggling to find respite of peace.

Looking for the sweetness of serenity.

I often go sit by the sea,

The calmness of it all is comforting.

Clear and blue,

Warm and cool.

No turbulence,

Waves flow smooth.

Waves rise high again and again,

Like the size of huge mountains.

With a little patience the waves will soon lessen.

Until the next storm comes again.

These are challenging times we're living in.

Sometimes you don't even see the waves coming in,

And then there's periods of calm once again.

Sea winds pierce into my solitude.

In a world that can be so cold,

These quiet moments,

Are like silk to the soul!

Ride the waves of life my friend,

From the beginning until the very end.

Part five

Coping / Acknowledging Divine Decree

How Wonderful Is The Affair Of The Believer
for his affairs are all good,
and this applies to no one but the believer.
If something good happens to him,
he is thankful for it and that is good for him.
If something bad happens to him,
he bears it with patience and that is good for him."
[Narrated by Muslim, 2999].

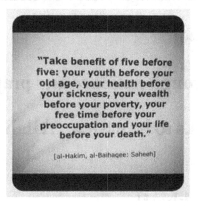

"Take benefit of five before five: your youth before your old age, your health before your sickness, your wealth before your poverty, your free time before your preoccupation and your life before your death."

[al-Hakim, al-Baihaqee: Saheeh]

- Loss brings lessons. Lessons bring new ways of looking at life. Realize that hardships are a part of life. You and your loved ones will experience trials many times and in many ways. Ask Allah what am I to learn through this? Find moments of beauty and joy in the depths of your anguish. Seek God and open your heart to His love and peace.

We all need time to heal and experience the feeling of grief as it comes. But, it is imperative to keep moving forward despite the loss. The process of bereavement carries you back to the past, reminding you of all that you could have said or done, and this makes you feel depressed and lonely. Try going back to your usual routine, this may serve as a healthy distraction to channel your energy to do something good. One is never really prepared for this paralyzing pain, yet Allah (glorified and exalted be He) reassures us that "For indeed with every hardship will be ease" [Surah 94 verse 5].

If you aid Allah's religion, Allah will aid you. "Indeed Allah will help those who help Him. Indeed Allah is Exalted in Might, All-Powerful."

[*Al-Qur'an* 22:40]

Seek help through patience and prayer. [2:45]

Whoever seeks to be patient, Allah will give him patience".

[Sahih Al-Bukhari]

Ibn 'Umar used to say, "If you survive till the evening, do not expect to be alive in the morning, and if you survive till the morning, do not expect to be alive in the evening, and take from your health for your sickness, and (take) from your life for your death." [Al-Bukhari #6416]

Take advantage of five blessings before deprived

Ibn Abbas reported: The Messenger of Allah, peace and blessings be upon him, said, **"Take advantage of five before five: your youth before your old age, your health before your illness, your riches before your poverty, your free time before your work, and your life before your death."**

Source: Shu'ab al-Imān 957 *Sahih* (authentic) according to Al-Albani

Abbas reported: I was riding behind the Messenger of Allah, peace and blessings be upon him, when he said to me, "Young man, I will teach you some words. Be mindful of Allah and he will protect you. Be mindful of Allah and you will find him before you. If you ask, ask from Allah. If you seek help, seek help from Allah. Know that if the nations gathered together to benefit you, they will not benefit you unless Allah has decreed it for you. And if the nations gathered together to harm you, they will not harm you unless Allah has decreed it for you. The pens have been lifted and the pages have dried." [Source: Sunan al-Tirmidhī 2516]

Grade: *Sahih* (authentic) according to Al-Tirmidhi

Umm Salamah (May Allah be pleased with her) said: When her husband Abu Salamah (May Allah be pleased with him) died, I repeated the same supplication as the Messenger of Allah (sallallahu 'alaihi wa sallam) had commanded me (to do). {('Inna lillahi wa inna ilaihi raji'un. Allahumma ujurni fi musibati, wakhluf li khairan minha}– Verily to Allaah we belong and to Him is our return. O Allaah, reward me in affliction and compensate me with something better' So Allah bestowed upon me a better substitute than him (i.e I was married to Muhammad, the Messenger of Allah (sallallahu 'alaihi wa sallam)). [Sahih Muslim 918, Riyaad as-Saaliheen, Book 7, Hadith 921]

Life is a gift from Allah. Our children, family, friends, neighbors, and even strangers are all gifts to be savored. Although some days may be full of hardship and sadness, with each breath & each heartbeat illustrates the beautiful gift of life. Keep the positive memories alive. Choose positive memories over regret, choose love over sorrow, forgiveness over anger, and peace over anxiety.

And thank God for the blessings in your past, present, and future.

THE PAUSE BUTTON

Nature has restorative qualities. Connect with nature. It is nurturing, beautiful, and a reminder of Allah's creations. It becomes easier to go inward and focus when you feel comfort, and you're not stressed.

*Anas Bin Malik reported: Whilst we were with the Messenger of Allah (sallallahu alayhi wa sallam) rain fell upon us. The Messenger then exposed part of his garment so that rain fell on his body. When we asked him why he did so, he replied **"Because it has just come from the Exalted Lord"**.*

CREATE FOR CALM

When you do something creative, you become relaxed and focused on the present activity and let go of spiraling thoughts. Be creative! Make something new, do a project, sew, knit, crochet, write, draw, paint, whatever it is you enjoy doing.

Dua's (supplications) are the biggest weapons of a Believer in Islam. While the believer is still alive, he/she makes Duas for our well-being, and now that he/she has gone to the afterlife, that person relies on our Dua since he/she desperately needs them now. Make Dua for the forgiveness of loved ones. Make Dua that they enter Jannah Al-Firdous.

Poems

BEGINNINGS AND ENDINGS

Beginnings and endings become intertwined,
By letting go of the past
And leaving some things behind.
A new beginning
Takes courage and confidence to be bold,
But, Embracing new beginnings,
Something new may unfold.
Change is both an end and a beginning.
One paints the canvas of the beginning of a certain end,
Or the newness of an uncertain beginning.
Beginnings and endings come at the same time.
Beginnings and Ending are always intertwined.

TO LIVE

I am learning how to live,
In a new way.
Ever since that fateful day,
You were taken away.

I am learning how to live
With things left unsaid,
Knowing there are so many words,
Unresolved in my head.

I am learning how to live
By embracing joyful times,
And the hurt and the pain.
Knowing that you live on,
Through the memories that remain.

I know that you're in Allah's care.
Knowing this gives me the strength to keep moving,
And makes the heartache much easier to bear.

EVERYTHING DUE TO ARRIVE
IS INDEED CLOSE

Do you see how the two renewables
Night and day.
Come and then go away?

With each night and day passing,
We see that this world is not everlasting!
Trust not in this world and its pleasures,
Paradise is the undisputed treasure.
Time is indeed perplexing,
In the way it passes by so quickly.
First you're here and then you're gone,
First you're surrounded by people
Then you're all alone.

Everything due to arrive is indeed close,
And death is closer than anything else
In yet, we fear it the most!.
Until your appointed time draws near,
Remember your Lord and worship Him
With love and fear!
It is Him we revere!
Today we are here,
Tomorrow we may not be,
So live your life righteously.
Everything due to arrive is indeed close,
Death is nearer than anything, and yet we fear it the most.

IN THE MIDST OF LIFE WE ARE
IN THE MIDST OF DEATH

Not simply because of the seeds of our physical decline,
Nor all the things we have left behind,
Or those people which have left us in the passage of time.
We consistently experience the smaller deaths of life,
We are always in the process of ending and beginning.
We all experience some forms of death eventually.
Sometimes slowly, other times swiftly.
There are gains and losses at every age,
In life there is always a turning of a page.
Change is both an ending and a beginning.
The canvas is painted of the beginning of a certain end,
Or the end of an uncertain beginning.
Sometimes changes come one at a time or cumulatively.

Beginnings and endings are intertwined,

And sometimes they're combined.

It's Life, Loss, and Love to Experience,

Be ready when each arrives.

BROKEN PIECES

She's had her share of a broken heart,

Break ups,

Break downs,

And breakthroughs.

Throughout her life she's seen at least a few.

All in an obscured view.

Some people say they felt the same way too.

No straight lines in her life,

The roads have curves and bends,

The roads haven't always been easy,

But so far no hopeless ends.

LET IT GO

For a while she wore gray like rain clouds,

Like a shadow that appears in between crowds.
Circumstances brought unexpected feelings of loss.
A sight, a sound, a scent, or a holiday,
Could trigger a sudden burst of sadness
And then it goes away.

She used her pen to release the shadows of grief,
Letting the sunshine dance beneath her feet.

Days may be filled with light,

As she untangled the layers of her life.

Yet that shadow remains just behind you.

Although we experience joy,

We feel our loved one absence too.

Her words explored emotional shadows,

Respecting them all until they were hallow.

When a large shadow looms low,

She embraces it patiently,

And then let's it go.

CHASING RAINBOWS

I'll paint you a rainbow
To hang on your wall
To brighten your heart when gray shadows fall.
I'll paint bright colors
That will make you smile,
I'll paint rainbows
Far and wide.
Your sorrow will soon disappear,
Replaced by a smile.
Happiness will be with you for a while.
Everything will be great,
All your sadness will soon abate.
Suspended over your head above,
You'll see a rainbow designed with love.

NOT BY CHANCE

No karma

No coincidence,

No soothsayer pretense.

Nothing ever happens by chance.

No wrong turn,

No victim of circumstance.

No mishap

No mistake,

No lucky break.

No horoscope

No astrological take.

Allah controls what is and what will be,

It's already written,

It's Divine Decree.

What is meant for you will not pass you by,

What isn't meant for you will pass you by.

Allah's foreknowledge

Doesn't compromise human responsibility,

We are held accountable for what is in our capability.

Almighty Allah's knowledge encompasses everything!

THE ROAD BACK TO YOURSELF

The time will come

When with joy and elation,

You will greet yourself

Arriving at your own door.

You will look in the mirror

And see your presence,

And your effervescence.

You will see who you were before,

And who you are now,

The traveled road back to yourself,

A new version of yourself.

Each self will smile and embrace

The other's welcome.

You will love the stranger who is your past self.

The one who has always loved you,

The one who has been there helping you.

You will hardly recognize her now,

But she always knew that one day

She would have to be let go,

For she has continued to grow and outgrow

Her old self.

We learn to love and honor ourselves,

And accept the things we've been through.

Love, loss, death,

All of these are true.

And in all of these is a healing to win the battle within you.

CREATE YOUR OWN STORY

Sometimes you have to let go

of what you thought your life would be at this time,

Accept the present circumstances & leave the past behind.

Find joy in the life you're actually living now.

And embrace life as it is right now.

Appreciate your joy with gratitude,
And give yourself moments of solitude.
Reflect on how much you have been given,
And how Allah has favored you.
You are blessed in everything you go through.
Remember the blessings that come every day.
Always enjoy the present,
Before time slips away.
Start your day with gratitude.
And end your day with gratitude.

WE STAND IN NEED OF ALLAH

Allah will dispel all your worries,
And remove any difficulties,
In life we all have a destiny,
A much deeper reality.
We all receive blessings continuously.
But when we're hurting,
We want relief immediately.
For pain makes you feel lost,
Full of vulnerability.
Ask Allah for guidance abundantly,
Strive to hold on to a victor mentality.
Recite the Qur'an,
And remember Allah daily.
Trust in Allah The Al-Mighty!
Call on Allah in times of ease and difficulty.
We are in need of Allah daily.

Abu Huraira reported: The Messenger of Allaah (Sallallahu alayhi wa sallam) said: The nearest a servant comes to his Lord is when he is prostrating himself, so make supplication (in this state). [Sahih Muslim]

IN PRAYER

She stayed in her private chambers

She prayed in the innermost part of the room.

Every time she prayed she renewed her commitment to Allah,

And she recited a generous amount of du'a.

Entreating and supplicating to her Lord,

And expressing all the things she's grateful for.

She stayed in her private chambers,

In her space of serenity.

Where she feels only love and tranquility.

Closing

Perhaps this humble effort will change your view on death and preparing for death; Or at least change your view on life. Life and death are intrinsically threaded. As I write, this I still hear of people fighting over wearing masks that would not only protect themselves but others from this virus covid-19. We should still be social distancing, limiting our contact with people outside of our homes, wearing a mask, and making every effort to keep ourselves safe as well as others. Many restaurants are closed for in-door dining, some offer take-out only, or have limits of 25% capacity. Many workers have been laid off and some businesses have been forced to shut down temporarily or in some cases permanently, unable to survive such a great monetary loss. We have now over 500,000 people, human beings, that have died from covid-19 and countless others who have been afflicted with this virus. This is a collective lost for the world and for many a deeply personal one. During this pandemic and before it, we have all dealt with loss and death, and yet will still recognize the many blessings we have to be thankful for. We must not lose hope or faith. We must be grateful for all we have, and all we have been given from our Lord. May Allah subhaanahu wa ta'aala accept my sincere effort and may the message of love, hope, resolution, and faith come across as intended. All praise to Allah! The Lord of all Creation.

When you wake up in the morning, be grateful to see another day. Another day to do better, be better, and worship your Lord. May Allah subhanahu wa ta ala keep our affairs in order, keep us firm and guided upon the haqq, and allow us to keep our tongue moist with His remembrance. Aameen. May Allah take our souls when He's most pleased with us and grant us the highest Jannah without reckoning Aameen

About The Author

Nailah Abdus-Salaam is a Believer, Writer, Educator and a Poetess. I enjoy teaching as well writing. So after 34 years as an educator in the E.O. school district, I used my creative skills as both a teacher and a writer to start writing poems and Some of my works published. I worked with middle school students "THE LONG JOURNEY". Most of her students participated and it was acknowledged and recognized with an award and plaque from the Superintendent of schools, as well as published in the local newspaper. I have previously written two other books that are published, and now this is my third book publication. "The BLESSINGS AND LOSSES WE SHARE". This latest book as well as the other two books can be purchased online at Barnes & Noble and on Amazon: https://www.amazon.com/

I've had articles featured in Essence, Azizah Magazine, & the Shahada Journal News. My poems are in several Anthologies of Poetry such as "BENEATH THE WINTER SKY" & THE STARS IN MY HEART" and several of my poems are published in the anthology "Scattered Petals". My poetry was also published in Best Poets and Poems which featured poets and poems selected by the editors of World Poetry Movement. I am also a published author on Timbooktu & was selected as the TimBookTu Featured Writer/Poet for Spring in 2017.

You can contact Ms. Abdus-Salaam via e-mail at nasintegrity@gmail.com